MEAL IN A MUG

80

FAST, EASY
RECIPES
FOR
HUNGRY
PEOPLE

ALL YOU NEED
IS A MUG AND A MICROWAVE

DENISE SMART

EBURY
PRESS

13 5 7 9 10 8 6 4 2

Published in 2014 by Ebury Press, an imprint of Ebury Publishing

A Random House Group Company

Text by Denise Smart © Ebury Press 2014
Photography by Howard Shooter © Ebury Press 2014

The Random House Group Limited Reg. No. 954009

Addresses for companies within the Random House Group can be found
at www.randomhouse.co.uk

A CIP catalogue record for this book is available from the British Library

The Random House Group Limited supports the Forest Stewardship Council® (FSC®), the leading
international forest-certification organisation. Our books carrying the FSC label are printed on
FSC®-certified paper. FSC is the only forest-certification scheme supported by the leading
environmental organisations, including Greenpeace. Our paper procurement policy can be found
at www.randomhouse.co.uk/environment

To buy books by your favourite authors and register for offers visit www.randomhouse.co.uk

Design: Smith & Gilmour
Photography and props: Howard Shooter
Food stylist: Denise Smart

Colour origination by Altaimage, London.
Printed and bound in China by C&C Offset Printing Co., Ltd

ISBN 978 0 091 95811 4

CONTENTS

INTRODUCTION

You like eating delicious food but don't have lots of fancy cooking equipment or much time to cook. Maybe you don't even have an oven. Or maybe you live on your own, or have just left home for the first time. Whether any of these scenarios describes you, or you're just looking for something different but easy for your mealtimes, then look no further: *Meal in a Mug* is the perfect book for you.

In the following pages, I'll prove to you that all you really need to make good food is a mug, a microwave, a handful of ingredients and a few basic utensils. Here you'll find 80 recipes that cover every mealtime, from breakfast, lunch and dinner to puddings, and those all-essential sweet or savoury snacks. Some of the recipes don't even require any cooking!

So whether you're a student on a budget, stuck at the office and starving, or just can't be bothered to dirty a saucepan and preheat the oven, you're sure to find some ideas to satisfy every hungry moment and all your flavour cravings. This book will show you that in the time it would have taken to cook that ready-meal or call your favourite takeaway delivery service, you could have created fresh, tasty food – from scratch.

THINGS YOU NEED TO KNOW ABOUT MICROWAVES...

When preparing food for microwave cooking, remember to follow these simple guidelines:

∗ **Important: all recipes in this book were tested in a 1000W, category-E microwave.**

∗ Microwave ovens vary, so you will need to adjust the cooking times accordingly. If unsure, check your machine's guidelines. A lower-wattage microwave will mean you'll need to cook food for slightly longer than the times given, but if that's the case, then it's best to add seconds, especially as it's very easy to overcook.

∗ You can always cook food for a little longer, but you won't be able to 'uncook' if you go too far. This is especially important when it comes to the Puddings and Baking chapter.

∗ Cut meat and vegetables into small, uniform sizes so that they cook evenly and quickly.

∗ Mugs will be hot when removed from the oven, so use oven gloves or a tea towel and be careful when handling them.

∗ If food is covered during cooking, be sure to make a small hole in the top of the cling film so steam doesn't build up and burn you when the covering is removed. Covering the food also helps to reduce splattering and helps it to cook more quickly.

∗ Most of the recipes say to allow for standing time once the food has been removed from the oven. This is so that the heat can continue to dissipate and finish cooking the food.

∗ Remember not to use any metal in the microwave, such as metal containers or foil.

∗ Stirring the food as recommended helps to ensure even cooking.

∗ Some of the recipes state to stand the mug in a shallow microwaveable bowl; this is to catch any liquid that may boil over, which will save you from having to clean the microwave afterwards.

∗ Remember, food cooked in a microwave will not brown, so some of the cakes and puddings may look slightly less appealing than if they had been baked in the oven. However, the flavours should be just as good.

THINGS YOU'LL NEED …

You don't need much but you will need the following:

Microwave Obviously.

Selection of mugs Follow the size of the mugs used in the recipes; otherwise food may boil over, or over- or undercook. It's useful to have about three different-sized microwaveable mugs: 500 ml/17 fl oz; 300 ml/½ pint; and 150–200 ml/5–7 fl oz.

Tea and coffee cups can also be used, especially for some of the puddings.

Measuring spoons A set of measuring spoons containing a ½ teaspoon (tsp), 1 teaspoon (tsp) and 1 tablespoon (tbsp) is essential. Unless otherwise stated, all spoon measures in the recipes are level.

Measuring jug For measuring larger quantities of liquid.

Fork and spoon Perfect for mixing and combining ingredients.

Kitchen scissors For cutting up ingredients such as meat, herbs and smaller vegetables.

Kettle For boiling water to dissolve stock cubes and jelly.

Sharp knife A small knife is useful for cutting up larger pieces of meat and vegetables, or peeling vegetables if you don't have a peeler.

Grater For grating cheese and removing the zest from citrus fruits.

INGREDIENTS TO BUY SO YOU'LL NEVER BE HUNGRY …

By keeping a selection of some of the following ingredients, you'll always be able to create a delicious meal. Any opened jars can be stored in the fridge once opened. Buy small tins of tomatoes and pulses so there will be less wastage; any leftover tinned food can be decanted into storage containers and kept in the fridge for a day or two.

FOR YOUR CUPBOARD

Sunflower and olive oil
Tinned chopped tomatoes
Tinned pulses, such as kidney
    beans, chickpeas
Tinned tuna or salmon
Tinned sweetcorn
Tinned pineapple
Tomato purée and ketchup
Soy sauce
Sweet chilli sauce
Ginger and garlic pastes
Dried herbs and spices, such as chilli
    powder, ground ginger, cumin,
    coriander, dried mixed herbs
Curry pastes, such a Moroccan,
    Thai and Indian
Packs of microwaveable rice
Long grain and risotto rice
Noodles: egg and rice
Selection of pasta shapes

Couscous
Chocolate: plain, milk and white
Tinned evaporated milk
Sugar: caster, light brown
Golden syrup, treacle and honey
Gravy granules and stock cubes
Flour: plain and self-raising
Baking powder
Bicarbonate of soda

FOR YOUR FRIDGE

Don't be tempted to buy too much fresh
food; if you can, plan what you want to eat
so that you don't end up with food spoiling.
If you have to buy bigger quantities of fresh
meat or fish, divide the remainder into
useable amounts and store in freezer-proof
bags, labelled and dated.
Chicken breasts
Minced beef
Chorizo
Bacon and ham
Salmon, cod, prawns
Milk
Butter
Cheese, such a Parmesan and Cheddar
Eggs
Crème fraîche, double cream
Fresh vegetables, such as peppers,
    onions, spring onions, new
    potatoes, sweet potatoes,
    carrots, mushrooms, tomatoes
Fresh pasta

TO KEEP IN THE FREEZER

Even if you have only a small freezer,
it is useful to have a few ingredients
such as the following stored away.
Remember to defrost meat and fish
thoroughly before using.
Frozen prawns
Frozen peas and spinach
Frozen berries, such
    as raspberries and
    mixed summer
Naan and pitta bread
Ice cream

Got all that? Now you're ready
to cook really fast, really tasty food.

BREAKFAST

EXTRA-CREAMY PORRIDGE

SERVES 1

Prep/cooking time: 3 minutes

Microwave: 1000W, category-E (see page 5)

5 tbsp porridge oats

200 ml/7 fl oz cold water

100 ml/3½ fl oz evaporated milk

Brown sugar, for sprinkling

This porridge is made really creamy by the addition of evaporated milk. You can substitute full-fat or semi-skimmed milk, though, if you don't have any evaporated milk to hand.

1 Put the oats in the bottom of a 500 ml/17 fl oz microwaveable mug or large cup and add the water. Stir, then microwave on high for 1 minute.

2 Remove from the microwave and stir in the evaporated milk. Return to the microwave and cook for a further minute. Stir well and allow to stand for 1 minute.

3 Serve sprinkled with sugar to taste.

PEANUT BUTTER AND JAM PORRIDGE

SERVES 1

Prep/cook time: 3 minutes

*Microwave: 1000W, category-E
(see page 5)*

5 tbsp porridge oats

200 ml/7 fl oz water

100 ml/3 ½ fl oz milk

1 tbsp crunchy peanut butter

½ tsp sugar

TO SERVE

1 tbsp strawberry jam

This might sound slightly unusual as you usually spread this combination on toast, but trust me: this porridge (pictured on page 8) tastes delicious!

1 Put the oats in the bottom of a 500 ml/17 fl oz microwaveable mug or large cup. Add the water. Stir, then microwave on high for 1 minute.

2 Remove from the microwave and stir in the milk. Return to the microwave and cook on high for 1 minute. Stir in the peanut butter and sugar and allow the mixture to stand for 1 minute before serving with a dollop of jam.

SCRAMBLED EGGS

SERVES 1

Prep/cook time: 2 minutes

Microwave: 1000W, category-E (see page 5)

Knob of butter

2 eggs

1 tbsp milk

Salt and freshly ground black pepper

TO SERVE

1 slice of toast

The trick to microwaving eggs is to cook them slowly; overcooking will result in rubbery scrambled eggs – no one wants this. Other than that, feel free to ad-lib: stir in any of your favourite fillings at the end.

1 Put the butter in the bottom of a 300 ml/ ½ pint microwaveable mug. Microwave on high for 20–30 seconds, until just melted.

2 Break in the eggs, add the milk and season with salt and freshly ground black pepper. Beat with a fork. Return to the microwave and cook on high for 30 seconds. Remove and break up the egg with the fork. Return to the microwave and cook on high for 10 seconds, and again, remove and break up with a fork. Repeat at 10-second intervals two more times.

3 Remove from the microwave and beat again; the eggs will still look runny in places, but they will continue to cook. Allow to stand for 1 minute, then serve with toast.

To make smoked salmon and chive scrambled eggs Stir in 1 tbsp chopped chives and a small handful of thinly sliced smoked salmon strips while the egg is still standing.

To make goats' cheese and tomato scrambled eggs Stir in 2 tbsp creamy goats' cheese and 8 cherry tomato halves.

EGGS FLORENTINE WITH HOLLANDAISE

SERVES 1

Prep/cook time: about 5 minutes

Microwave: 1000W, category-E (see page 5)

2 heaped tbsp butter

1 egg yolk

2 tsp fresh lemon juice

Salt and freshly ground black pepper

Large handful of spinach

1 egg

TO SERVE

1 slice wholemeal toast

Hollandaise sauce is so simple to make in the microwave. This recipe makes more hollandaise than you'll need for one portion. Double the rest of the recipe and share this excellent breakfast with a friend, or cover the sauce and keep it in the fridge for 2–3 days to serve cold.

1 To make the hollandaise sauce, put the butter in a small microwaveable cup and microwave on high for 10 seconds, until softened but not melted. Meanwhile, beat together the egg yolk and lemon juice in a small cup and allow to stand for 1 minute. Add to the softened butter.

2 Cook on high for 10 seconds, then beat well with a fork; the mixture may look slightly lumpy but any lumps will disappear on whisking. Repeat twice more until the sauce is smooth and has thickened. Season to taste.

3 Fill a large 500 ml/17 fl oz microwaveable mug with the spinach (it may seem like a lot but it will cook down). Cover with cling film and pierce the film with a knife, then microwave on high for 2 minutes until wilted.

4 Meanwhile boil the kettle and pour the water to come halfway up a 150 ml/¼ pint microwaveable mug. Break in the egg, then microwave on low power for 20 seconds and repeat for 10–20 seconds more until the egg is cooked to your liking.

5 Place the spinach on the slice of toast, then top with the egg. Spoon over a little hollandaise sauce and serve.

BREAKFAST MUFFIN

SERVES 1

Prep/cook time: 5 minutes

Microwave: 1000W, category-E (see page 5)

Butter, for greasing

4 tbsp self-raising flour

½ tsp ground mixed spice

1 tbsp mixed seeds

2 tbsp caster sugar

2 tbsp mashed banana

1 egg white, lightly beaten

2 tbsp sunflower oil

2 tbsp buttermilk or milk

12 fresh blueberries

This muffin is perfect for breakfast – it's packed with juicy blueberries, seeds and banana. You can have it cold if you need to eat on the go, but it's especially delicious served warm.

1 Lightly butter the inside of a 300 ml/ ½ pint microwaveable mug.

2 Put the flour, mixed spice, seeds and sugar in the bottom of the mug and stir to mix well.

3 In a small jug, beat the mashed banana with the egg white, oil and buttermilk or milk, then stir into the dry ingredients in the mug, making sure you have mixed in all the flour from the bottom of the mug.

4 Carefully stir in the blueberries. Stand the mug in a shallow microwaveable bowl as some of the blueberries may burst during heating and dribble down the sides.

5 Microwave on high for 2 ½ minutes, until risen and spongy, then allow to stand for 1 minute before serving.

BREAK-FEAST

SERVES
1

Prep/cook time: about 5 minutes

*Microwave: 1000W, category-E
(see page 5)*

1 tsp sunflower oil

3 cocktail sausages

3 mushrooms, quartered

1 rasher smoked back bacon,
trimmed of fat and chopped

1 x 150 g/5 ½ oz tin baked
beans in tomato sauce

TO SERVE

1 slice buttered toast

*Here's a complete breakfast in a mug. Although
sausages don't brown in the microwave, once
they're coated in the sauce used here, you'll
never know.*

1 Pour the oil in the bottom of a 500 ml/17 fl oz
microwaveable mug. Stir in the sausages and
mushrooms and cook on high for 1 minute.

2 Add the bacon and cook on high for 1 minute.
Stir in beans, cover with cling film and pierce
the film with a knife. Cook on high for 1 minute,
stir, then cover again and cook for 1 minute more.

3 Let it stand for 1 minute before serving with
a slice of buttered toast.

BACON AND TOMATO MUFFIN

Prep/cook time: about 7 minutes

Microwave: 1000W, category-E (see page 5)

1 tbsp melted butter, plus extra for greasing

1 rasher smoked back bacon, chopped

4 tbsp self-raising flour

3 tbsp finely grated Cheddar cheese

3 sun-dried tomatoes, chopped

1 tbsp chopped chives

100 ml/3 ½ fl oz buttermilk or milk

1 egg, beaten

Pinch of salt and freshly ground black pepper

This savoury muffin is delicious served warm and makes a satisfying breakfast or brunch. Pair it up with a Vanilla Latte (page 124) for your first meal of the day.

1 Lightly butter the inside of a 500 ml/17 fl oz microwaveable mug. Put the bacon in the bottom and cook on high for 1 minute. Stir to break up the bacon.

2 Add the flour, 2 tbsp of the cheese, the sun-dried tomatoes and chives and stir well. Add the buttermilk or milk, melted butter, egg and seasoning and mix well with a fork until all the ingredients are combined. Sprinkle the top with the remaining cheese.

3 Microwave on high for 4 minutes, then allow to stand for 1 minute. Turn out of the mug and allow to cool slightly before eating.

SERVES 1

SMOKED HADDOCK KEDGEREE

Prep/cook time: about 4 minutes

Microwave: 1000W, category-E (see page 5)

2 tsp medium curry paste

3 tbsp water

125 g/4½ oz cooked microwaveable pilau rice

1 tsp softened butter

4 tbsp small chunks smoked haddock: about 50 g/2 oz

1 tbsp freshly chopped parsley

2 tsp lemon juice

1 egg

Freshly ground black pepper

While kedgeree is perfect for breakfast, this spicy, smoky classic also makes a tasty lunch or supper dish – so feel free to make it whenever you like.

1 Mix the curry paste with 1 tablespoon of the water in the bottom of a 300 ml/½ pint microwaveable mug. Add the rice and butter and stir well.

2 Gently stir in the fish and remaining water. Cover with cling film and pierce the film with a knife. Cook on high for 1 minute.

3 Remove from the microwave and stir in the parsley and lemon juice. Make a well in the centre of the rice and break in the egg. Cover again with cling film and microwave on high for 1–1½ minutes, until the egg is just cooked.

4 Allow it to stand for 1 minute, then serve with freshly ground black pepper.

BIRCHER MUESLI

SERVES 1

*Prep time: 5 minutes,
plus soaking time*

4 tbsp porridge oats

1 small apple, grated

175 ml/6 fl oz milk

1 tbsp chopped almonds

2 tbsp fresh raspberries

2 tbsp fresh blueberries

TO SERVE

Scattering of mixed seeds

Honey or maple syrup

*Mix up the ingredients the night before and you'll
have a delicious breakfast ready the next morning.
Try adding a selection of dried fruits instead of
fresh for a texture treat.*

1 Mix everything together in a 300 ml/½ pint cup
or mug. Cover and place in the fridge for 1–2 hours
or overnight, so that the oats absorb the liquid.

2 Stir before serving and add a little extra milk
if you prefer a runnier consistency. Sprinkle
with the seeds and drizzle with some honey
or maple syrup and grab your spoon!

GRANOLA

SERVES
2

Prep/cook time: 3 minutes

Microwave: 1000W, category-E (see page 5)

2 tbsp honey

1 tbsp oil

Pinch of salt

1 tsp ground cinnamon

11 tbsp jumbo porridge oats

12 almonds

1 tbsp mixed seeds

2 tbsp raisins

TO SERVE

Fresh fruit

Yogurt

Honey

This is so simple to make. Add your favourite dried fruits, such as cranberries, blueberries or chopped apricots. This recipe serves two, but any leftover granola can be stored in an airtight container for up to one week.

1 Place 1 tbsp of the honey, all the oil, salt and cinnamon in the bottom of a 500 ml/17 fl oz microwaveable mug. Microwave on high for 30 seconds.

2 Add the oats and stir to coat them in the honey mixture. Microwave on high for 1 minute, then stir in the almonds and seeds.

3 Microwave on high for 1 minute and stir again. Stir in the remaining honey and the raisins and allow to cool.

4 Serve with fresh fruit, yogurt and a drizzle of honey for a real early morning treat.

HUEVO RANCHERO

SERVES 1

Cook/prep time: 3 minutes

Microwave: 1000W, category-E
(see page 5)

1 soft corn tortilla

3 tbsp fresh salsa

1 egg

1 tbsp freshly chopped coriander

Huevos rancheros, or 'ranch-style eggs', have become an international favourite and they're really easy to make. With a spicy hit of Mexican salsa, this egg recipe is quick to cook and uses just a few simple ingredients.

1 Cut the tortilla into 4 triangles and place these in the base and sides of a 200 ml/7 fl oz microwaveable coffee cup.

2 Spoon over the salsa. Cover with cling film and pierce with a knife, then microwave on high for 1 minute.

3 Remove from the microwave and make a well in the salsa. Crack in the egg.

4 Cover again with the cling film, then return to the microwave and cook on low for 1 minute for a soft yolk. Stand for 1 minute before sprinkling with the coriander and serving. If you prefer a harder yolk, cook for a further 30 seconds before letting it stand.

PRAWN LAKSA

SERVES
1

Prep/cook time: 5 minutes

Microwave: 1000W, category-E
(see page 5)

Large handful (50 g/2 oz)
flat dried rice noodles

100 ml/3½ fl oz fish stock

1 tbsp laksa paste

3 tbsp coconut cream

½ tsp fish sauce

6 cooked shelled king prawns

Small handful bean sprouts

8 tinned bamboo shoots, drained

1 tbsp freshly chopped coriander

TO SERVE

1 spring onion, chopped

½ red chilli, finely sliced

Laksa is a spicy, fragrant, coconut noodle soup. If prawns aren't your thing, replace them with a handful of cooked shredded chicken and change the fish stock to chicken stock (pictured on page 26).

1 Break the noodle sticks in half and put them in a 500 ml/17 fl oz microwaveable mug. Add the fish stock and stir, then microwave on high for 1 minute. Stir well.

2 Stir in the laksa paste, coconut cream and fish sauce and microwave on high for 1 minute.

3 Stir in the prawns, bean sprouts and bamboo shoots and microwave on high for 1 minute, or until the prawns are heated through. Stir in the coriander.

4 Top with the spring onions and chilli to serve.

PEA AND PESTO SOUP

SERVES 1

Prep/cook time: 6 minutes

Microwave: 1000W, category-E (see page 5)

2 medium new potatoes, peeled and chopped into 2 cm/¾-inch pieces

1 spring onion, chopped

200 ml/7 fl oz hot vegetable stock

6 tbsp frozen peas

1 tsp pesto sauce

TO SERVE

Sliced baguette

You can use pesto from a jar or chilled fresh pesto to make this simple soup. For a bit more texture, try scattering the top with a little crumbled feta on top.

1 Put the potatoes and spring onion in the bottom of a 500 ml/17 fl oz microwaveable mug. Add 3 tbsp of the stock, cover with cling film, pierce the top with a knife and microwave on high for 2 minutes, until tender. Stir in the peas and cover and cook on high for 1 minute.

2 Stand the mug in a shallow microwaveable dish, in case any liquid boils over. Stir in the remaining stock, cover again with the cling film and cook on high for 2 minutes, or until the peas are tender.

3 Mash the peas and potatoes with a fork until roughly crushed, or use a stick blender if you have one. Stir in the pesto.

4 Serve with a sliced baguette.

SMOKED HADDOCK CHOWDER

SERVES 1

Prep/cook time: about 5 minutes

*Microwave: 1000W, category-E
(see page 5)*

1 tsp oil

1 tbsp chopped onion

1 rasher smoked back
bacon, chopped

1 small potato, peeled and
cut into 1 cm/½-inch cubes

100 ml/3½ fl oz water

100ml/3½ fl oz milk

4 tbsp tinned sweetcorn, drained

4 tbsp skinless smoked
haddock pieces

Handful of baby spinach leaves

Freshly ground black pepper

TO SERVE

Crusty bread

Satisfying and warming, this chowder is a creamy soup that combines smoky bacon and smoked haddock for a rich, hearty flavour.

1 Pour the oil in the bottom of a 500 ml/17 fl oz microwaveable mug. Add the onion and bacon and cook on high for 30 seconds.

2 Add the potato and the water and cook on high for 2 minutes. Add the milk, sweetcorn and haddock and cook for 1 minute. Stir gently and cook on high for a further 30 seconds–1 minute, or until the fish starts to flake and the potatoes are tender.

3 Stir in the spinach, and allow to stand for 1 minute. Season to taste with freshly ground black pepper and serve with crusty bread.

CHORIZO AND BUTTER BEAN SALAD

SERVES 1

Prep/cook time: 3 minutes

Microwave: 1000W, category-E (see page 5)

1 small cooking chorizo sausage, cut into rings: about 4 tbsp

200 g/7 oz tinned butter beans in water, drained and rinsed

6 cherry tomatoes, halved

1 tsp sherry vinegar

2 tsp freshly chopped parsley

Freshly ground black pepper

TO SERVE

Crusty bread

This is so quick to prepare, and the paprika oil from the chorizo and the sherry vinegar make a perfect 'instant dressing'.

1 Put the chorizo in the bottom of a 300 ml/½ pint microwaveable mug and cook on high for 1 minute, until the oil is released.

2 Stir in all the remaining ingredients except the parsley and black pepper, return to the microwave and cook on high for 30 seconds. Stir again and add the parsley.

3 Season with freshly ground black pepper and serve with a chunk of crusty bread.

GOATS' CHEESE BASIL AND TOMATO QUICHE

SERVES 1

Prep/cook time: 3 minutes

Microwave: 1000W, category-E (see page 5)

2 eggs

2 tbsp milk

Salt and freshly ground black pepper

4 basil leaves, roughly torn

4 sun-dried or cherry tomatoes, halved

2 tbsp chopped goats' cheese

1 tbsp finely grated Parmesan

TO SERVE

Handful of rocket leaves

This is a healthier option than a traditional quiche made with a pastry base, but it's just as tasty. Serve it with a rocket salad for a quick, satisfying lunch.

1 Break the eggs into a 300 ml/½ pint microwaveable coffee cup. Add the milk and seasoning and beat together thoroughly, then stir in the basil, tomatoes and goats' cheese. Sprinkle the Parmesan over the top.

2 Cook on high for 2 minutes. Remove and allow to stand for 1 minute before serving with a handful of rocket leaves.

PESTO ORZO SALAD

SERVES 1

Prep/cook time: about 8 minutes

Microwave: 1000W, category-E (see page 5)

4 tbsp orzo pasta

150 ml/¼ pint boiling water

2 tbsp fresh pesto sauce

4 cherry tomatoes, halved or quartered

4 mini mozzarella balls or pearls, torn in half

1 tbsp toasted pine nuts

Handful of rocket leaves

Orzo is a tiny pasta that looks like rice. In this simple salad it is combined with the Italian flavours of tomatoes, mozzarella and basil.

1 Put the orzo in the bottom of a 500 ml/17 fl oz microwaveable mug. Add 50 ml/2 fl oz of the water and microwave on high for 2 minutes. Stir well to break up the pasta, than add another 50 ml/2 fl oz of water and microwave on high for 2 minutes.

2 Remove from the microwave and stir in the remaining water, then place back in the microwave and cook on high for 1 minute. Stir well and allow to stand for 2 minutes, then stir in the pesto sauce.

3 Add the tomatoes, mozzarella and pine nuts and stir in the rocket leaves. Serve immediately.

COUSCOUS WITH MINT, FETA AND POMEGRANATE

SERVES 1

4 tbsp couscous

Boiling water

Grated zest and juice of ½ lemon

4 roasted sweet piquanté red peppers, from a jar, halved

3 tbsp crumbled feta cheese

3 tbsp pomegranate seeds

1 tbsp freshly chopped mint

1 tsp olive oil

Salt and freshly ground black pepper

TO SERVE

Pitta bread

This refreshing salad is perfect for a light lunch. Serve with pitta bread.

1 Put the couscous in the bottom of a 500 ml/17 fl oz mug and add enough boiling water to cover. Cover with cling film and leave to stand for 3–4 minutes, or until the water has been absorbed.

2 Fluff the couscous with a fork, then stir in the lemon zest and juice and allow to cool. Stir in the peppers, cheese, pomegranate seeds, mint and oil. Season to taste and stir well.

3 Serve immediately with pitta bread.

REFRIED BEAN WRAP

SERVES
1

Prep/cook time: 3 minutes

Microwave: 1000W, category-E
(see page 5)

3 tbsp tinned refried beans

1 tortilla wrap

1 spring onion, chopped

3 green jalapeño peppers, optional

1 tbsp chopped fresh coriander

2 tbsp fresh tomato salsa

4 tbsp grated Cheddar or
Mexican-style Cheddar

Vary the ingredients here to suit your tastes – try it with cooked shredded chicken, for instance, but remember to keep the cheese and salsa so that it holds together. Top it with some soured cream and guacamole for a more substantial meal. This is best eaten with a fork, accompanied by some crisp salad leaves.

1 Spread the beans over the base of the tortilla wrap, leaving a 2-cm/¾-inch border. Sprinkle it with the spring onions, jalapeños (if using) and coriander, top with the salsa and sprinkle in the cheese.

2 Fold over the edges of the tortilla, then roll it up from the bottom to securely encase the ingredients.

3 Place in a tall, narrow mug and microwave on high for 1½ minutes (don't worry if the tortilla collapses slightly). Allow it to stand for 1 minute before serving.

THAI BEEF NOODLE SALAD

SERVES 1

Prep/cook time: 5 minutes

Microwave: 1000W, category-E (see page 5)

1 nest of instant rice vermicelli noodles

Boiling water

small chunk of cucumber

1 small carrot, peeled and cut into thin strips

1 spring onion, finely chopped

1-2 slices cooked roast beef, cut into thin strips

Small handful of freshly chopped coriander

1 tbsp dry-roasted peanuts, chopped, optional

FOR THE DRESSING

Juice of 1 small lime

2 tbsp Thai sweet chilli sauce

2 tsp light soy sauce

If time permits, allow this salad to stand for about 10–15 minutes in order to allow the flavours to develop. Otherwise, you can simply prepare it in advance, then cover and refrigerate it until ready to eat.

1 Put the noodles in the bottom of a 500 ml/17 fl oz mug, (you may have to break the nest in half). Cover with boiling water and allow to stand for 3 minutes. Drain in a sieve and rinse under cold running water, then drain well.

2 Meanwhile, cut the cucumber in half lengthways, then scoop out the seeds with a teaspoon and discard them. Slice the flesh thinly.

3 In the bottom of the mug, mix together the dressing ingredients, then add the noodles and stir to coat well. Add the cucumber, carrot, spring onion, beef and coriander. Toss together using 2 forks until all the ingredients are coated in the dressing.

4 Sprinkle with the peanuts, if using, and serve.

MISO CHICKEN NOODLE SOUP

SERVES 1

Prep/cook time: 5 minutes

Microwave: 1000W, category-E (see page 5)

1 tsp miso paste

½ tsp ginger paste
or chopped ginger

300 ml/½ pint hot chicken stock

1 nest of fine egg noodles

Small handful shredded
cooked roast chicken

1 spring onion, chopped

2 tbsp fresh or frozen
edamame beans

This healthy Japanese-inspired soup is aromatic and filling – just perfect for a speedy, nutritious lunch.

1 Put the miso paste and ginger in the bottom of a 500 ml/17 fl oz microwaveable mug. Pour in the stock and stir well.

2 Add the noodles and place the mug in a shallow microwaveable bowl, in case any of the liquid should boil over. Cook on high for 2 minutes.

3 Remove from the microwave, stir well, then add the chicken, spring onion and beans. Microwave on high for 1 minute, or until the chicken and beans are heated through.

4 Allow to stand for 1 minute, then serve.

SPICY LENTIL AND BACON SOUP

SERVES 1

Prep/cook time: about 10 minutes

Microwave: 1000W, category-E (see page 5)

1 tsp sunflower oil

1 rasher smoked back bacon, chopped

2 tbsp chopped onion

½ tsp ground cumin

¼ tsp ground turmeric

1 small carrot, peeled and diced

4 tbsp split red lentils

300 ml/½ pint hot chicken or vegetable stock

Pinch of dried chilli flakes

TO SERVE

Naan bread

Dried red lentils are a perfect ingredient to keep in your cupboard. As well as for hearty soups, you can use them to make tasty curries such as dhals.

1 Put the oil, bacon, onion, cumin and turmeric in a 500 ml/17 fl oz microwaveable mug, stir well and cook on high for 1 minute. Stir in the carrot and lentils.

2 Add 100 ml/3½ fl oz of the stock and stand the mug in a shallow microwaveable bowl. Cook on high for 2 minutes. Stir and microwave on high for a further 2 minutes.

3 Stir in another 100 ml/3½ fl oz of the stock and add the chilli flakes. Cook on high for 2 minutes.

4 Stir in the remaining stock and cook on high for 1 minute, until the lentils are tender. Stand for 1 minute and serve with naan bread.

SNACKS AND SIDES

SERVES 1

POPCORN

Prep/cook time: 2 minutes

Microwave: 1000W, category-E
(see page 5)

2 tsp sunflower oil

2 tbsp popping corn

Salt or sugar, for sprinkling, optional

The hardest part of making your own popcorn (pictured on page 44) is choosing the flavour. Once you've decided, take two minutes to make a batch before you settle down to watch that film...

1 Pour the oil in the bottom of a 500 ml/17 fl oz microwaveable mug. Add the corn and cover the mug with cling film. Pierce a small hole in the film with a knife.

2 Microwave on high for 1 minute. Using a tea towel or oven gloves (the mug will get hot!), remove from the microwave and shake the mug.

3 Return to the microwave and cook on high for a further minute. Remove from the microwave and allow to stand for 1 minute.

4 Sprinkle with a little salt or sugar, if using, and enjoy!

To make spiced smoked paprika popcorn: prepare the popcorn as in the basic recipe above. While the popcorn is standing, mix together 1 tsp smoked paprika, ½ tsp ground cumin, ½ tsp ground black pepper and a pinch of salt in a small cup. Sprinkle the spices over the top of the warm popcorn and drizzle with 1 tsp olive oil. Cover the mug again and shake it well so all of the popcorn is well-coated. Serve immediately.

To make cocoa and marshmallow popcorn: prepare the popcorn as in the basic recipe above, but using 1 tsp oil and 1 tbsp popping corn. Allow to stand for 1 minute, then add 1 tbsp drinking chocolate and 2 tbsp marshmallows then stir well.

LEMON AND CHILLI WEDGES

SERVES 1

Prep/cook time: 5 minutes

Microwave: 1000W, category-E (see page 5)

1 medium sweet potato, scrubbed and cut into small wedges

3 wedges lemon

1 small red chilli, deseeded and fincly choppcd, optional

1 tbsp freshly chopped coriander

Salt and freshly ground black pepper

½ tsp olive oil

These wedges won't crisp up like oven-baked ones, but they're still delicious. If you prefer, roughly crush the potatoes with the back of a fork.

1 Stand the potato wedges in a tall 500ml/17 fl oz microwaveable mug. Add the lemon wedges.

2 Cover with cling film and pierce the film with a knife, then microwave on high for 4 minutes. Allow to stand for 1 minute, then carefully remove the lemon wedges with a fork and squeeze the juice from them over the potatoes. Scatter on the chilli, if using, then the coriander. Season and drizzle with the olive oil before serving.

CHEESY NACHOS

SERVES 1

Cooking time: 1 minute

Microwave: 1000W, category-E (see page 5)

---

12 original-flavour tortilla chips

2–3 tbsp tomato salsa

2 tbsp grated Cheddar cheese

6 sliced jalapeño peppers

TO SERVE

Soured cream and or guacamole

Cheaper than the restaurant equivalent, and so quick to prepare, this is another great sofa snack.

1 Layer about 6 tortilla chips in the base and sides of a 300 ml/ ½ pint microwaveable coffee cup.

2 Spoon over 1 tbsp of salsa, 1 tbsp of grated cheese and a few jalapeños, then repeat the layers, finishing with the cheese.

3 Microwave on high for 1 minute.

4 Serve topped with a little soured cream or guacamole.

EGG FRIED RICE

Prep/cook time: 5 minutes

Microwave: 1000W, category-E
(see page 5)

125 g/4½ oz cooked long grain
microwave rice

2 tbsp frozen peas

1 small slice ham, diced

1 spring onion, chopped

Small handful of bean sprouts

1 egg

1 tsp light soy sauce

½ tsp sesame oil

*This rice makes a perfect accompaniment to any
Chinese dish. Alternatively, why not make it into
a main meal by adding some cooked peeled prawns?*

1 Put the rice in the bottom of a 300 ml/½ pint
microwaveable mug. Cover with cling film,
pierce the film with a knife and microwave
on high for 1 minute.

2 Stir in the peas, ham, spring onion and bean
sprouts, cover again and cook on high for 1 minute.

3 In a small bowl, beat the egg with the soy and
sesame oil. Add this mixture to the mug and stir
into the rice. Cover again with the cling film and
cook on high for 30 seconds. Stir, then allow it
to stand for 1 minute before serving.

GARLICKY MUSHROOMS

SERVES 1

Prep/cook time: 3 minutes

Microwave: 1000W, category-E (see page 5)

20 button mushrooms

1 garlic clove, crushed

1 tsp softened butter

1 tbsp freshly chopped parsley

Salt and freshly ground black pepper

TO SERVE

Bread or toasted brioche

This is an indulgent snack, especially when served on a slice of toasted brioche.

1 Put the mushrooms, garlic and butter in the bottom of a 300 ml/½ pint microwaveable mug. Cover with cling film and pierce the film with a knife. Microwave on high 1 minute.

2 Stir well, then return to the microwave and cook on high for 30 seconds. Stir in the parsley and season to taste.

3 Serve with some bread or toasted brioche to mop up the garlic butter.

CAULIFLOWER CHEESE

SERVES 1

*Prep/cook time: 6 minutes, plus
3–4 minutes standing time*

*Microwave: 1000W, category-E
(see page 5)*

1 tbsp butter

1 tbsp plain flour

150 ml/¼ pint milk

½ tsp Dijon mustard

3 tbsp finely grated Gruyère cheese

8 small cauliflower florets

Salt and freshly ground
black pepper

*This cauliflower cheese is made using Gruyère,
which adds a nutty flavour, but you can always
use a mature Cheddar if you like. Serve as a meal
on its own or as an easy side dish.*

1 Put the butter, flour and milk in the bottom of a
500 ml/17 fl oz microwaveable mug. Cook on high
for 30 seconds, then whisk. Return to the microwave
and cook for another 30 seconds, then whisk again.
Repeat until the sauce thickens. Don't be tempted
to ignore the 30-second intervals or the sauce may
go lumpy!

2 Stir in the mustard and the cheese and stir until
the cheese melts, then add the cauliflower and stir
to coat in the cheese sauce. Cover the mug with cling
film and pierce, return it to the microwave and cook on
medium for 3–4 minutes, until the cauliflower is tender.

3 Allow to stand for 3–4 minutes before serving,
as the sauce will be very hot.

ROSEMARY, GARLIC POTATOES

SERVES 1

Prep/cook time: about 4 minutes

Microwave: 1000W, category-E (see page 5)

2 tsp softened butter

1 garlic clove, crushed

5 baby new potatoes

1 tsp freshly chopped rosemary

Salt and freshly ground black pepper

These delicious potatoes are so quick to cook you'll hardly believe you've made them yourself. You could substitute some freshly chopped thyme for the rosemary for a flavour change.

1 Put the butter and garlic in the bottom of a 300 ml/½ pint microwaveable cup or mug. Microwave on high for 30 seconds.

2 Stir in the potatoes and rosemary and season well, then stir to coat the potatoes in the garlic butter. Cover with cling film and pierce with a knife.

3 Microwave on high for 2–3 minutes, or until the potatoes are tender. Allow to stand for 1 minute before serving.

HONEYED CARROTS

SERVES 1

Prep/cook time: 3 minutes

Microwave: 1000W, category-E (see page 5)

7 baby Chantenay carrots

1 tsp butter

1 tsp honey

Salt and freshly ground black pepper

Give your carrots a slightly sweet taste with the addition of honey for this simple but elegant side dish.

1 Put the carrots, butter, honey and seasoning in a 500 ml/17 fl oz microwaveable mug. Microwave on high for 2 minutes.

2 Stir well, then microwave on high for a further minute, or until the carrots are just tender.

3 Allow to stand for 1 minute before serving.

POTATO DAUPHINOISE

SERVES 1

Prep/cook time: 6 minutes

Microwave: 1000W, category-E (see page 5)

Butter, for greasing

100 ml/3 ½ fl oz double cream

1 tbsp milk

1 garlic clove, crushed

1 tsp freshly chopped rosemary

Salt and freshly ground black pepper

2 small potatoes, peeled and very thinly sliced

This rich and indulgent French potato recipe makes a wonderful side dish, but it's delicious enough to eat as a meal on its own.

1 Lightly butter the inside of a 300 ml/½ pint microwaveable mug.

2 In a small jug, stir together the cream, milk, garlic and rosemary. Season well.

3 Place a couple of layers of potatoes in the bottom of the mug and pour in a little of the cream mixture; continue layering and pouring over a little more of the cream until the potatoes are about 2.5 cm/1 inch from the top of the mug. Finish with any remaining cream mixture.

4 Cover the mug with cling film and pierce the top with a knife. Stand the mug in a microwaveable shallow bowl in case any of the mixture boils over. Cook on medium for 4–5 minutes, or until a knife goes easily through the potatoes.

5 Allow to stand for 1 minute before serving.

CORNBREAD

Prep/cook time: 4 minutes

Microwave: 1000W, category-E (see page 5)

2 tbsp plain flour

2 tbsp coarse cornmeal or polenta

½ tsp baking powder

Pinch of salt and freshly ground black pepper

1 spring onion, chopped

1 red chilli, deseeded and chopped (optional)

2 tbsp tinned sweetcorn

125 ml/4 fl oz buttermilk or milk

1 tbsp melted butter

1 egg

Cornbread is soft and moist, so allow it to cool slightly before slicing it into rounds. It makes a perfect accompaniment to Chilli con Carne (see page 78) or any of the soup recipes (see pages 28–30). For cornbread with a kick, add a chopped red chilli.

1 In a 500 ml/17 fl oz microwaveable mug, mix together the flour, cornmeal, baking powder, seasoning, spring onion, chilli (if using) and sweetcorn.

2 In a jug, whisk together the buttermilk or milk, melted butter and egg and stir into the dry ingredients in the mug. Mix well until all the ingredients are combined.

3 Microwave on high for 2 minutes. Allow to stand for 1 minute, then turn out and serve.

FRUITY COUSCOUS

SERVES 1

Prep/cook time: 5 minutes

Microwave: 1000W, category-E (see page 5)

4 tbsp couscous

Boiling water

Finely grated zest and juice of ½ lemon

2 tbsp toasted pine nuts

2 tbsp raisins or sultanas

1 spring onion, finely chopped

1 tbsp freshly chopped parsley

This couscous makes a perfect partner for the Sweet Potato and Chickpea Tagine on page 86, but it also makes a satisfying sweet-savoury snack on its own.

1 Put the couscous in the bottom of a 300 ml/½ pint mug and pour in enough boiling water to cover. Cover the mug with cling film and leave to stand for 3–4 minutes, or until the water has been absorbed.

2 Fluff the couscous with a fork, then stir in the lemon zest and juice, pine nuts, raisins or sultanas, spring onion and parsley. Serve immediately.

CHOCOLATE PEANUT BUTTER COOKIE

SERVES 1

Prep/cook time: about 3 minutes

Microwave: 1000W, category-E (see page 5)

1 tbsp softened butter

2 tsp crunchy peanut butter

2 tbsp soft brown sugar

Pinch of salt

¼ tsp vanilla extract

1 egg yolk

1 tsp milk

3 tbsp plain flour

2 tbsp dark or milk chocolate chips

Craving a cookie, but don't fancy baking a whole batch? Then just follow this recipe for a quick fix. Serve it warm with a scoop of chocolate or vanilla ice cream.

1 Put the butter and peanut butter in the bottom of a 300 ml/½ pint microwaveable coffee mug or teacup. Microwave on high for 30 seconds, then remove and stir the mixture until completely melted.

2 Stir in the sugar, salt, vanilla extract, egg yolk and milk, then add the plain flour and stir until the mixture is well combined.

3 Add the chocolate chips and mix until the chips are evenly distributed. Flatten the top with the back of a spoon.

4 Microwave on high for 40–50 seconds, until the dough is just cooked. Allow it to stand for 1 minute so that the cookie finishes cooking.

CHEESE AND CHIVE SCONEBREAD

SERVES 2

Prep/cook time: 4 minutes

Microwave: 1000W, category-E (see page 5)

4 tbsp plain flour

½ tsp baking powder

¼ tsp mustard powder

¼ tsp salt

Freshly ground black pepper

Pinch of cayenne pepper

2 tbsp butter, cut into small pieces

3 tbsp finely grated mature Cheddar cheese

1 tbsp chopped chives

½ beaten egg

2 tbsp milk

This would be the perfect partner for a bowl of steaming soup. Use a chopped spring onion instead of the chives if that's all you have in the fridge. Spread the sconebread with a little butter and eat it while it's still warm.

1 Put the flour in a wide 300 ml/ ½ pint microwaveable mug or cup (this makes it easier to rub in the butter – see below). Stir in the baking powder, mustard, seasoning and cayenne.

2 Using your fingertips, rub in the butter until the mixture resembles fine breadcrumbs, then stir in most of the cheese (reserving a little for the top) and the chives.

3 Add the egg and milk and mix together with a fork until all the ingredients are incorporated and you have a sticky dough. Sprinkle with the reserved cheese and cook on high for 1½ minutes. Allow to stand for 1 minute.

4 Turn out of the cup and cut into slices.

CHOC-CHIP MUFFINS

SERVES 2

Prep/cook time: 5 minutes

Microwave: 1000W, category-E (see page 5)

4 tbsp self-raising flour

4 tbsp soft light brown sugar

1 tbsp cocoa powder

2 tbsp lightly whisked egg white

½ tsp vanilla extract

3 tbsp milk

3 tbsp sunflower oil

3 tbsp dark chocolate chips

These chocolatey muffins are best served warm. To make things even easier, you could also mix all the ingredients together in a 300 ml/ ½ pint cup to create one large muffin.

1 Put 2 paper muffin cases in the base of 2 x 200 ml/ 7 fl oz microwaveable coffee cups, or line them with parchment paper.

2 In a small bowl or jug, mix together the flour, sugar, cocoa powder, egg white, vanilla extract and 1 tbsp of the milk to make a smooth paste.

3 Stir in the remaining milk, all of the oil and 2 tbsp of the chocolate chips.

4 Divide the chocolate mixture between the 2 cases, then sprinkle the top with the remaining chocolate chips.

5 Microwave on high for 3 minutes. Remove and allow to stand for 1 minute before serving.

MAINS

CHICKEN KORMA

SERVES 1

Prep/cook time: about 8 minutes

Microwave: 1000W, category-E
(see page 5)

1 small skinless chicken breast,
cut into small pieces

½ tsp garlic paste

½ tsp ginger paste

½ tsp hot chilli powder

½ tsp tomato purée

½ tsp ground coriander

¼ tsp ground turmeric

2 tbsp ground almonds

2 cardamom pods, lightly crushed

4 tbsp natural full-fat yogurt

1 tbsp cream

½ tsp garam masala

2 tbsp flaked almonds

TO SERVE

Naan bread or rice

For stronger flavours, marinate the chicken for two to three hours or overnight in the fridge if you wish. Serve it with a warm ready-made naan bread, or stir in some cooked rice and microwave on high for 1 minute (pictured on page 64).

1 Put all the ingredients, except the cream, garam masala and flaked almonds, in a large 500 ml/17 fl oz microwaveable mug. Mix well. Stand the mug in a shallow microwaveable bowl in case any mixture overflows. Cover with cling film.

2 Pierce the cling film with a knife and cook on high for 2 minutes. Stir well, then return to the microwave and cook on low for 4 minutes.

3 Stir in the garam masala, cream and flaked almonds and allow to stand for 1 minute before serving with naan bread or rice.

THAI PRAWN CURRY

SERVES 1

Prep/cook time: 8 minutes

Microwave: 1000W, category-E (see page 5)

1 tbsp Thai red or green curry paste

½ lemon grass stalk, roughly chopped

2 lime leaves, shredded

200 ml/7 fl oz coconut milk

4 baby corn, halved

4 green beans, cut into 2 cm/¾-inch pieces

100 g/3½ oz frozen or fresh, peeled, cooked prawns

6 tbsp microwave Thai rice, cooked

TO SERVE

Freshly chopped coriander

This aromatic curry is cooked in coconut milk that has been infused with lemon grass and lime leaves. Choose between red or green curry paste – green is usually slightly hotter.

1 In a large 500 ml/17 fl oz microwaveable mug, stir together the curry paste, lemon grass, lime leaves and coconut milk. Microwave on high for 2 minutes.

2 Stir in the baby corn and green beans and cook on high for 2–3 minutes, or until just tender.

3 Add the prawns, stir well and cook on high for 2 minutes if frozen or 1 minute if fresh.

4 Add the rice and cook on high for 1 minute. Stir well and serve immediately with freshly chopped coriander sprinkled on top.

PANCETTA AND DOLCELATTE RISOTTO

SERVES 1

Prep/cook time: about 11 minutes

Microwave: 1000W, category-E (see page 5)

1 tsp olive oil

2 tbsp cubed pancetta

1 tbsp chopped onion

1 tsp garlic paste

4 tbsp arborio rice

400 ml/14 fl oz hot chicken stock

2 tbsp chopped dolcelatte cheese or other creamy blue cheese

Large handful of baby spinach leaves

Freshly ground black pepper

This simple supper dish is full of flavour. You could add any creamy blue cheese, such as Gorgonzola, but don't be tempted to add more salt, as the pancetta and cheese are already quite salty.

1 Put the oil, pancetta, onion and garlic paste in the bottom of a large 500 ml/17 fl oz microwaveable mug and cook on high for 1 minute.

2 Stir in the rice and pour over 100 ml/3½ fl oz of the stock. Stand the mug in a shallow microwaveable bowl (just in case any liquid boils over) and microwave on high for 2 minutes. Stir, then pour in another 100 ml/3½ fl oz of the stock and cook on high for 2 minutes. Repeat until all the stock has been used up and the rice is just tender.

3 Stir in the dolcelatte and spinach and leave to stand for 1 minute, until the spinach has wilted. Season to taste with freshly ground black pepper and serve immediately.

SERVES 1

WILD MUSHROOM RISOTTO

Cooking time: about 10 minutes,
plus 10 minutes soaking time
for the mushrooms

Microwave: 1000W, category-E
(see page 5)

2 tbsp dried wild mushrooms

400 ml/14 fl oz hot chicken
or vegetable stock

4 tbsp arborio rice

1–2 tbsp freshly grated
Parmesan cheese

1 tbsp freshly chopped
flatleaf parsley

Salt and freshly ground
black pepper

Truffle oil, to drizzle, optional

Dried mushrooms are a great store-cupboard standby and are packed full of flavour. This risotto uses only a few ingredients, but it tastes delicious.

1 Put the mushrooms in a large 500 ml/17 fl oz microwaveable mug. Add 100 ml/3½ fl oz of the stock. Leave to soak for 10 minutes.

2 Stir in the rice. Stand the mug in a shallow microwaveable bowl (just in case any liquid boils over) and microwave on high for 2 minutes. Stir, then pour over 50 ml/2 fl oz of the stock and cook for 1 minute. Repeat until all the stock has been used up and the rice is just tender.

3 Stir in the Parmesan and parsley and leave to stand for 1 minute. Season to taste and serve immediately with a drizzle of truffle oil, if using, and more freshly ground black pepper.

SPAGHETTI CARBONARA

Prep/cook time: 9-10 minutes

Microwave: 1000W, category-E (see page 5)

2 rashers smoked streaky bacon, chopped

1 garlic clove, crushed

22 sticks spaghetti, broken into pieces

150 ml/¼ pint boiling water

4 tbsp light cream cheese

2 tbsp milk

2 tbsp freshly grated Parmesan cheese

1 tbsp freshly chopped parsley

Freshly ground black pepper

A classic Italian favourite, this dish is traditionally cooked using eggs and single cream. However, this recipe is slightly healthier because it uses reduced-fat cream cheese instead.

1 Put the bacon and garlic in the bottom of a large 500 ml/17 fl oz microwaveable mug and cook on high for 1 minute. Remove and stir to break up the bacon.

2 Add the spaghetti and water and microwave on high for 1 minute, then stir well. Return to the microwave and cook on medium for a further 2 minutes.

3 Stir in the cream cheese and milk and cook on high for 2 minutes. Stir and cook for a further 2 minutes, or until the pasta is just cooked.

4 Stir in the Parmesan and parsley. Stand for 1 minute before serving with freshly ground black pepper.

SERVES 1

MACARONI CHEESE

Prep/cook time: about 14 minutes

Microwave: 1000W, category-E
(see page 5)

4 tbsp dried macaroni

175 ml/6 fl oz cold water, plus 2 tbsp

2 tbsp soft cream cheese

¼ tsp English mustard

2 tbsp grated mature
Cheddar cheese

Salt and freshly ground
black pepper

Truffle oil, to drizzle (optional)

*Presenting the ultimate comfort food: pasta coated
in a tangy cheese sauce. You can make this even more
delectable by drizzling it with a little truffle oil.*

1 Put the macaroni in the base of a large 500 ml/17 fl oz
microwaveable mug. Add 75 ml/3 fl oz of the water. Put
the mug in a shallow microwaveable bowl (some of the
water will boil over) Cover with cling film, pierce the film
with a knife and microwave on high for 2 minutes.

2 Stir well, pour any of the water in the bowl back into
the mug, then add another 50 ml/2 fl oz of the water and
microwave for a further 2 minutes. Repeat the process
2 more times, or until the pasta is just tender: about
8 minutes in total.

3 Stir in a further 2 tablespoons of water, the cream
cheese, mustard and grated Cheddar. Return to the
microwave and cook on high for 2 minutes.

4 Stir well, then season to taste with salt and freshly
ground black pepper and leave to stand for 1 minute.
Serve with a little truffle oil, if desired.

To make macaroni with mustard, ham and spinach Cook 4 tbsp
of dried macaroni as above, then stir in the remaining water, 2 tbsp
cream cheese, 1 tsp wholegrain mustard, a handful of baby spinach
leaves and 1 slice of ham, chopped. Cook for a further 2 minutes.
Season to taste and stand for 1 minute before serving.

TOMATO PASTA WITH COURGETTES

SERVES 1

Prep/cook time: 6 minutes

Microwave: 1000W, category-E (see page 5)

1 garlic clove, crushed

½ small courgette, diced

40 pieces fresh fusilli pasta (125 g/4½ oz)

100 ml/3½ fl oz boiling water

4 tbsp passata with peppers and chilli

2 tbsp mascarpone cheese

2 basil leaves, shredded

TO SERVE

Freshly ground black pepper

Green salad

Crusty bread

Fresh pasta cooks really quickly in the microwave. Some penne pasta would work well here, too, if you want something other than fusilli.

1 Put the garlic, courgette and pasta in a large 500 ml/ 17 fl oz microwaveable mug. Pour over the boilling water and stir. Cover with cling film and pierce the film with a knife.

2 Stand the mug in a shallow microwaveable bowl (as some of the water may boil over) and cook on high for 2 minutes. Remove and stir well, then stir in the passata and mascarpone, cover again with the film and cook on medium for 2 minutes, or until the pasta is just cooked.

3 Stir in the basil and allow to stand for 1 minute before serving with freshly ground black pepper, a crisp green salad and crusty bread.

SPAGHETTI BOLOGNESE

SERVES 1

Prep/cook time: 10 minutes

Microwave: 1000W, category-E (see page 5)

½ tsp olive oil

2 tbsp chopped onion

3 tbsp minced beef

4 mushrooms, chopped

1 x 227 g tin chopped tomatoes

½ tsp dried mixed herbs

8 strands spaghetti, broken into pieces

Salt and freshly ground black pepper

TO SERVE

1 tbsp grated Parmesan cheese

This Italian classic is ridiculously easy to prepare in a mug using only a few ingredients.

1 Place the oil, onion and minced beef in the bottom of a 500 ml/17 fl oz microwaveable mug. Stir well, then microwave on high for 1 minute.

2 Remove and break up the mince with a fork. Stir in the mushrooms, tomatoes, herbs, spaghetti and seasoning.

3 Stand the cup in a shallow microwaveable bowl (in case any of the mixture boils over) and cook on high for 2 minutes. Remove, stir well and cook on high for a further 2 minutes.

4 Stir again and cook for a further 2 minutes, or until the spaghetti is cooked. Allow to stand for 1 minute before serving with the Parmesan.

CHILLI CON CARNE

SERVES 1

Prep/cook time: 6 minutes

Microwave: 1000W, category-E (see page 5)

1 tsp sunflower oil

2 tbsp chopped onion

4 tbsp minced beef

1 tsp chilli powder, or to taste

½ tsp cocoa powder

4 tbsp chopped tomatoes

1 x 227g tin red kidney beans, drained and rinsed

Salt and freshly ground black pepper

6 tbsp cooked microwave long grain rice

TO SERVE

Soured cream

Cornbread (see page 58)

This well-known spicy meal is sure to become a midweek favourite. Try it served with homemade Cornbread on page 58.

1 Put the oil, onion and mince in the bottom of a 500 ml/17 fl oz microwaveable mug. Cook on high for 1 minute, then stir with a fork to break up the mince.

2 Add the chilli, cocoa powder, tomatoes and kidney beans and cook on high for 2 minutes.

3 Season to taste and stir well, then put the rice on top. Cover with cling film and pierce the top with a knife. Microwave on high for 1 minute. Stir the rice into the chilli mixture and let it stand for 1 minute.

4 Serve with a dollop of soured cream and a slice of cornbread.

SPINACH AND RICOTTA LASAGNE

SERVES 2

Prep/cook time: 10 minutes

Microwave: 1000W, category-E (see page 5)

8 portions (nuggets) frozen spinach

2 large fresh lasagne sheets

Boiling water

4 tbsp ricotta cheese

1 tbsp pine nuts, optional

½ tsp ground nutmeg

Salt and freshly ground black pepper

2 tbsp passata

6 tbsp ready-made chilled cheese sauce

1 tbsp freshly grated Parmesan cheese

TO SERVE

Crisp green salad

Lasagne for two is so simple to make. Use coffee cups; they're wider than mugs and allow for more even cooking.

1 Put the spinach in a microwaveable cup. Cover with cling film, pierce the film with a knife and microwave on high for 3 minutes.

2 Cut each lasagne sheet into 6 portions and place in a shallow bowl. Pour over enough boiling water to cover and leave for 30 seconds–1 minute, until softened. Drain.

3 Mix the spinach with the ricotta, pine nuts, nutmeg and seasoning. Put 1 tbsp of the passata in the base of each of 2 x 300 ml/½ pint microwaveable coffee cups.

4 Add 2 pieces of lasagne to each cup. Don't worry if they go up the sides of the cup.

5 Add half the spinach mixture and 1 tbsp of the cheese sauce to each, then add another 2 sheets of lasagne and the remaining ricotta mixture. Top with the remaining lasagne sheets, then spoon over the remaining cheese sauce, spreading it to cover the lasagne.

6 Sprinkle with the Parmesan, then place the cups in the microwave and cook on high for 4 minutes, until bubbling.

7 Allow to stand for 2 minutes before serving with a crisp green salad.

JAMBALAYA WITH PRAWN AND CHORIZO

Prep/cook time: about 15 minutes

Microwave: 1000W, category-E (see page 5)

2 tbsp chopped chorizo sausage

1 tbsp chopped onion

4 tbsp long grain rice

300 ml/½ pint hot chicken stock

4 tbsp chopped tinned tomatoes

1 tsp dried mixed herbs

¼ each small red and green peppers, deseeded and cubed

2 tbsp frozen peas

6 cooked and peeled king prawns

1 spring onion, chopped

Dash of Tabasco sauce, optional

This lightly spiced Cajun rice dish originated in Louisiana in the USA. If you prefer, replace the prawns with some diced chicken breast; just add it to the mug when you stir in the rice.

1 Put the chorizo and onion in the bottom of a 500 ml/ 17 fl oz microwaveable mug. Cook on high for 1 minute, until the paprika oil is released from the sausage.

2 Stir in the rice until coated in the oil. Add 100 ml/ 3½ fl oz of the stock and cook on high for 2 minutes. Stir in another 100 ml/3½ fl oz of stock and microwave on high for 2 minutes.

3 Stir in the tomatoes and herbs. Stand the mug in a shallow microwaveable bowl and microwave on high for 3 minutes.

4 Remove and stir in 50 ml/2 fl oz of the stock and cook on low for 3 minutes.

5 Stir in another 50 ml/2 fl oz of stock and the peppers and cook on low for 2 minutes.

6 Stir in the peas, prawns and spring onion, (reserve a few onions for garnish), and cook on high for 2 minutes, or until the rice is tender and most of the liquid has been absorbed. Add a dash of Tabasco, if using, and serve garnished with the reserved spring onion.

CHICKEN STEW WITH HERBY DUMPLINGS

SERVES 1

Prep/cook time: about 11 minutes

*Microwave: 1000W, category-E
(see page 5)*

2 tbsp chopped onion

1 small carrot, peeled and chopped into 1 cm/½-inch pieces

1 small potato, peeled and chopped into 1 cm/½-inch pieces: about 2–3 tbsp

200 ml/7 fl oz hot chicken stock

2 tsp chicken flavour gravy granules

Handful of shredded cooked chicken (about 50g/2 oz)

Pinch of dried mixed herbs or 2 tsp freshly chopped parsley

FOR THE DUMPLINGS

2 tbsp self-raising flour

1 tbsp suet

½ tsp dried mixed herbs

4 tsp water

A comforting Sunday lunch all in one mug. Follow this up with a Sticky Toffee Pudding for a complete meal (page 106).

1 Put the vegetables in the bottom of a 500 ml/17 fl oz microwaveable mug. Add 100 ml/3½ fl oz of the stock and stand the mug in a shallow microwaveable dish. Cover the mug with cling film and pierce the film with a knife. Cook on high for 2 minutes.

2 Remove and stir, then cover and return to the microwave and cook on high for 2 minutes.

3 Meanwhile, in a small cup mix together all the ingredients for the dumplings. Stir the remaining stock, gravy granules, chicken and herbs into the vegetables in the mug.

4 Using a spoon, divide the dumpling mixture into 2 and dollop both on top of the stew. Cover again with the cling film and microwave on high for 1–1½ minutes, or until the dumplings are just set.

5 Allow to stand for 2–3 minutes before serving.

SWEET POTATO AND CHICKPEA TAGINE

SERVES 1

Prep/cook time: about 10 minutes

Microwave: 1000W, category-E (see page 5)

1 tsp oil

1 tbsp chopped onion

½ tsp garlic paste

1 tsp ras el hanout Moroccan spice blend

¼ sweet potato, peeled and chopped into 2 cm/¾-inch pieces: about 100 g/3½ oz

100 ml/3½ fl oz vegetable stock or water

4 tbsp tinned chopped tomatoes

4 ready-to-eat dried apricots, chopped

3 tbsp tinned chickpeas

½ tsp harissa paste

2 green olives, sliced

TO GARNISH

4 almonds

½ preserved lemon, pith removed and cut into thin strips, optional

TO SERVE

Fruity Couscous (page 59)

This healthy vegetarian Moroccan stew is packed full of flavour. Serve with plain couscous or Fruity Couscous (see page 59). The preserved lemon adds a lovely citrus flavour; thankfully, preserved lemons are easy to buy nowadays in most supermarkets.

1 Put the oil, onion, garlic and spice blend in a 500 ml/ 17 fl oz microwaveable mug and cook on high for 1 minute. Stir in the sweet potato and 50 ml/2 fl oz of the stock or water. Cover with cling film and pierce the film with a knife.

2 Cook on high for 2 minutes. Stir well, then cook on high for a further 2 minutes, until the potato is just tender.

3 Stir in the tomatoes, apricots, chickpeas and the remaining stock or water. Microwave on medium for 3 minutes.

4 Stir in the harissa paste and olives and allow to stand for 1 minute. Garnish with the almonds and preserved lemon, if using, and serve with Fruity Couscous (see page 59).

SALMON AND PARSLEY FISH PIE

SERVES
1

Prep/cook time: about 7–9 minutes

Microwave: 1000W, category-E (see page 5)

1 tbsp butter

2 tbsp plain flour

150 ml/¼ pint milk

1 tbsp crème fraîche
or double cream, optional

2 tbsp freshly chopped parsley

Salt and freshly ground
black pepper

1 small skinless salmon fillet, cubed

2 tablespoons frozen peas

6 heaped tbsp chilled
mashed potato

A little grated cheese, optional

Substitute your favourite fish for the salmon – cod or smoked haddock would work well – or add some cooked peeled prawns.

1 Put the butter, flour and milk in the bottom of a large 500 ml/17 fl oz microwaveable mug. Cook on high for 30 seconds, then whisk.

2 Return the mug to the microwave and cook for another 30 seconds, then whisk again. Repeat until the sauce thickens. Don't be tempted to ignore the 30-second intervals or the sauce may go lumpy!

3 Stir in the crème fraîche or cream (if using) and parsley and season to taste. Add the fish and peas, then top with the mashed potato and sprinkle with the cheese, if using.

4 Stand the mug in a microwaveable bowl, as some of the sauce may boil over. Cook on low for 3–4 minutes, or until the fish is cooked. Allow to stand for 2 minutes before serving.

SPICY LAMB MEATBALLS

SERVES
1

Prep/cook time: about 9 minutes

Microwave: 1000W, category-E
(see page 5)

4 tbsp minced lamb

½ tsp ground cumin

½ tsp ground coriander

2 tsp freshly chopped coriander,
plus extra to garnish

Salt and freshly ground
black pepper

5 tbsp tinned chopped tomatoes
with chilli

¼ red pepper, deseeded
and cut into thin strips

TO SERVE

A little freshly chopped coriander

Flatbreads and/or couscous

*These Middle Eastern-inspired meatballs are
ridiculously easy to prepare and cook. They're also
delicious served with Fruity Couscous (page 59),
or flatbreads and maybe a spoonful of yogurt.*

1 Mix together the mince, spices and fresh coriander
and season well. Using your hands, mix the ingredients
together, then roll between your palms to make
6 small meatballs.

2 Place in the bottom of a 300 ml/½ pint microwaveable
mug. Cover with cling film and pierce the film with a knife.

3 Microwave on high for 1 minute. Stir in the tomatoes
and red pepper, cover again and cook on medium for
3 minutes. Stir, cover again and return to the microwave
and cook on medium for 1 minute.

4 Stand for 1 minute, then garnish with a little chopped
coriander. Serve with couscous and flatbread, if desired.

SWEET-AND-SOUR CHICKEN

SERVES 2

Prep/cook time: 10 minutes

Microwave: 1000W, category-E
(see page 5)

4 tsp cornflour

1 large boneless, skinless chicken
breast, cut into small cubes

½ red pepper, deseeded
and cut into cubes

2 spring onions, chopped

1 x 150 g sachet straight-to-wok
medium noodles

FOR THE SAUCE

1 x 227 g tin pineapple
pieces, in natural juice

2 tbsp tomato ketchup

1 tbsp soft light brown sugar

1 tbsp dark soy sauce

1 tbsp white wine vinegar

1 tsp ginger paste

1 tsp garlic paste

Cold water

Cook this Chinese favourite in less time than it takes to order from your local takeaway! There are quite a lot of ingredients, but don't let that put you off: most are store-cupboard staples.

1 First, make the sauce. Drain the juice from the pineapple into a measuring jug, and reserve 2 tbsp of juice and 4 tbsp of the pineapple pieces. Stir in the ketchup, sugar, soy sauce, vinegar and pastes. Make up to 250 ml/9 fl oz with cold water.

2 Add 2 tsp of the cornflour and 1 tbsp of the reserved pineapple juice to each of 2 x 500 ml/17 fl oz microwaveable mugs; stir well. Divide the chicken, red pepper and spring onions between the mugs and mix well.

3 Divide the sauce between the 2 mugs, stir well and cook on high power for 2 minutes. Stir in the reserved pineapple pieces, cover with cling film and pierce the film with a knife.

4 Return the mugs to the microwave and cook on low for 4 minutes. Stir well. Break the noodles in half, add half to each mug, cover and cook on low for 2 minutes.

5 Stir well and allow to stand for 1 minute before serving.

BEEF COBBLER

Prep/cook time: about 8 minutes

Microwave: 1000W, category-E (see page 5)

1 tsp oil

1 tbsp chopped onion

4 tbsp minced beef

3 tsp gravy granules

150 ml/¼ pint boiling water

½ carrot, chopped

2 small new potatoes, quartered

2 tbsp frozen peas

FOR THE COBBLER

2 tbsp softened butter

4 tbsp self-raising flour

2 tbsp milk

This hearty meal makes a perfect Sunday lunch. Use a cup rather than a mug to make it; otherwise the cobbler will sink.

1 Put the oil, onion and mince in the bottom of a 300 ml/ ½ pint microwaveable cup.

2 Cook on high for 1 minute, then stir with a fork to break up the mince. Mix the gravy granules with the boiling water in a small cup.

3 Add the carrot, potatoes and gravy to the mince, stir well and stand the cup in a shallow microwaveable bowl, as some of the liquid will boil over. Cover with cling film and pierce the film with a knife.

4 Cook on medium for 2 minutes. Add the peas, stir well, cover again with the cling film, then return to the microwave and cook on medium power for 1 minute, until the vegetables are just tender.

5 Meanwhile, make the cobbler. In a small cup or bowl, rub the butter into the flour, then mix together with the milk to form a slightly sticky dough.

6 Divide the dough into two pieces, roll into balls and flatten slightly. Arrange over the top of the mince, cover the cup with cling film, pierce the film with a knife, then return to the microwave and cook on medium for 2 minutes.

7 Allow to stand for 2 minutes before serving.

PUDDINGS AND BAKING

CHOCOLATE AND PISTACHIO BROWNIE

SERVES 1

Prep/cook time: 1 minute

Microwave: 1000W, category-E (see page 5)

2 tbsp plain flour

2 tbsp soft brown sugar

1 tbsp cocoa powder

Pinch of salt

1 tbsp sunflower oil

2 tbsp milk

1 tbsp chopped pistachios

1 tbsp dark or milk chocolate chips

This delicious brownie (pictured on page 92) is slightly gooey on the inside. You can substitute any chopped nuts, such as macadamias, for the pistachios if you prefer. Served warm with a scoop of ice cream.

1 In a 200 ml/7 fl oz microwaveable cup or mug, mix together the dry ingredients, then stir in the oil and milk until you have a smooth batter with no lumps. Stir in the nuts and chocolate chips.

2 Microwave on high for 1 minute.

WHITE CHOCOLATE, LIME CHEESECAKES

SERVES 2

Prep/cook time: about 4 minutes, plus 30 minutes chilling time

Microwave: 1000W, category-E (see page 5)

2 tbsp softened butter

4 dark chocolate digestive biscuits, crushed

75 g/3 oz good-quality white chocolate, broken into small pieces

Finely grated zest of 1 small lime

250 g/9 oz mascarpone cheese

1 tbsp icing sugar, sifted

TO DECORATE

Grated lime zest

Grated white chocolate

This no-cook cheesecake is a breeze to make. The creamy, tangy filling is complemented by a chocolatey biscuit base.

1 Put 1 tbsp of the butter in each of 2 x 200 ml/7 fl oz microwaveable teacups. Microwave on high for 30 seconds-1 minute, or until the butter has melted. Divide the biscuit crumbs between the cups and mix with the melted butter, then press down with the back of a spoon. Place in the fridge to set while you make the filling.

2 In a small microwaveable bowl, melt the chocolate on medium for 1 minute, stir, then microwave in 30-second intervals until melted. Stir well, then beat in the lime zest, mascarpone and icing sugar.

3 Spoon the mixture over the biscuit base and chill in the refrigerator for 30 minutes, or until set. Decorate with a little grated lime zest and grated chocolate.

LEMON PUDDING

SERVES 1

Prep/cook time: 3 minutes, plus 4 minutes standing time

Microwave: 1000W, category-E (see page 5)

FOR THE SPONGE

1 tbsp softened butter

3 tbsp caster sugar

Finely grated zest of 1 lemon

3 tbsp milk

3 tbsp self-raising flour

½ beaten egg

FOR THE SAUCE

2 tbsp boiling water

1 tsp softened butter

2 tbsp soft brown sugar

Juice of 1 lemon

This pudding separates into two layers, a light sponge and a tangy sauce, as it cooks in minutes.

1 To make the sponge, put the butter in the bottom of a large 500 ml/17 fl oz microwaveable mug. Melt on high for 30 seconds. Stir in the caster sugar, lemon zest, milk, flour and egg and beat until smooth.

2 To make the sauce, pour the boiling water in a small jug. Add the butter, stir until melted, then stir in the sugar and lemon juice. Carefully pour the sauce over the sponge mixture, then microwave on high for 2 minutes, or until just cooked in the centre.

3 Stand for 4 minutes before serving, as the sauce will be extremely hot.

AFFOGATO AL CAFFE

SERVES 2

Prep time: 2 minutes

4 scoops good-quality
vanilla ice cream

2 freshly made espresso coffees
(made with espresso powder
or with an espresso machine,
if you're feeling flashy)

TO SERVE
2 amaretti biscuits

*Hot coffee over cold ice cream, this must be
the simpliest dessert in the world to make.*

1 Scoop 2 balls of the ice cream into each
of 2 cappuccino cups or latte glasses.
Pour a cup of hot coffee quickly over each.

2 Serve immediately, with the biscuits
on the side for dunking.

RASPBERRY AND ELDERFLOWER JELLIES

SERVES 2

Prep/cook time: 3 minutes, plus
40 minutes chilling time.

Microwave: 1000W, category-E
(see page 5)

6 cubes raspberry jelly,
cut into small pieces

100 ml/3½ fl oz boiling water

200 ml/7 fl oz sparkling elderflower
pressé, chilled

14 frozen raspberries

Serve these pretty jellies in glass cups or small glass latte mugs. You can easily double the recipe to make four – perfect for entertaining! Using frozen raspberries makes the jelly set even quicker.

1 Put the jelly in the bottom of a microwaveable measuring jug, add the boiling water and stir until the jelly has dissolved. If the jelly does not dissolve thoroughly, put it in the microwave and cook on high for 30 seconds.

2 Once all the jelly has dissolved, stir in the elderflower pressé and raspberries. Divide between 2 x 200 ml/ 7 fl oz glass mugs or cups and place in the refrigerator for about 40 minutes, or until set.

BERRY CRUMBLE

SERVES 1

Prep/cook time: 3 minutes

Microwave: 1000W, category-E (see page 5)

125 g/4½ oz mixed frozen berries (raspberries, blueberries or redcurrants)

1 tsp soft brown sugar

1 tsp cornflour

FOR THE CRUMBLE

4 tbsp whole rolled porridge oats

2 tsp brown sugar

¼ tsp ground cinnamon

1 tsp butter, melted

TO SERVE

Vanilla ice cream or custard

A really simple, delicious crumble that you can adapt with any of your favourite frozen berries, such as raspberries or blueberries.

1 Put the berries in a 150 ml/¼ pint microwaveable mug; they should almost come up to the top. Sprinkle the sugar and cornflour over them and microwave on high for 30 seconds. Stir gently so you don't break up the berries, then microwave on high for another 30 seconds, or until the sauce starts to thicken.

2 Put the oats in a small cup or bowl and stir in all the remaining crumble topping ingredients. Spoon the crumble over the berries and stand the cup in a microwaveable shallow bowl, in case any of the sauce bubbles over. Microwave on high for 1 minute 20 seconds.

3 Allow to stand for 1 minute before serving with a scoop of vanilla ice cream or custard.

TOFFEE AND BANANA PUDDING

SERVES 2

Prep/cook time: 5 minutes

Microwave: 1000W, category-E (see page 5)

FOR THE TOFFEE SAUCE

2 tbsp butter

4 tbsp soft brown sugar

2 tbsp evaporated or full-fat milk

FOR THE SPONGE

1 ripe banana

3 tbsp plain flour

¼ tsp baking powder

¼ tsp bicarbonate of soda

2 tbsp soft brown sugar

½ tsp vanilla extract

1 egg, beaten

1 tbsp milk

1 tbsp sunflower oil

10 pecans, broken into pieces

Banana and toffee make a perfect combination, and this recipe is also a great way of using up over-ripe bananas. It's delicious served with cream.

1 First, make the toffee sauce. Put the butter, sugar and milk in a small microwaveable cup or bowl and microwave on high for 30 seconds. Stir, then microwave for a further 30 seconds.

2 Put the banana in a small bowl and mash it with a fork. Stir in all the remaining sponge ingredients.

3 Divide half the toffee sauce between 2 x 300 ml/ ½ pint microwaveable mugs, then divide the banana mixture between the mugs.

4 Microwave on high for 2½ minutes. Allow to stand for 1 minute, then pour the remaining toffee sauce over the top and serve.

MELTING CHOCOLATE PUDDINGS

SERVES
2

Prep/cook time: about 3 minutes

Microwave: 1000W, category-E
(see page 5)

4 tbsp dark chocolate chips

2 tbsp softened butter

2 tbsp caster sugar

½ tsp vanilla extract

1 tbsp plain flour

1 egg, beaten

*These delicious chocolatey puddings have a gooey
centre. They're delicious served with a scoop of vanilla
or pistachio ice cream – a good bake for date night.*

1 Put the chocolate chips and butter in a small
microwaveable bowl or large mug and microwave
on high for 1 minute. Remove and stir, then return
to the microwave and cook on high for 20–30 seconds,
or until the butter and chocolate are completely
melted. Stir well.

2 Stir in the sugar, vanilla, flour and egg and keep
stirring until all the ingredients are combined.

3 Divide the mixture equally between 2 x 150 ml/
¼ pint microwaveable cups or mugs and cook
on high for 40–50 seconds.

4 Allow to stand for 1 minute before serving.

STICKY GINGERBREAD

SERVES 2-4

Prep/cook time: 5 minutes,
plus cooling

Microwave: 1000W, category-E
(see page 5)

2 tbsp softened butter, plus extra
for greasing

4 tbsp treacle

4 tbsp dark muscovado sugar

2 tbsp milk

¼ tsp bicarbonate of soda

1 piece of stem ginger, from a jar,
chopped, plus reserve 2 tbsp of
the ginger syrup

1 tsp ground ginger

½ tsp ground cinnamon

8 tbsp plain flour

1 egg, beaten

This recipe is a great idea for Bonfire Night. If you have time, make it the day before and wrap it in foil to keep it moist.

1 Lightly butter the sides of 2 x 300 ml/ ½ pint microwaveable mugs and line the bases with baking paper.

2 Put the butter, treacle and sugar in a microwaveable jug and microwave on high for 2 minutes, until the mixture is boiling.

3 Add the milk and bicarbonate of soda, then stir in the stem ginger, spices, flour and egg. Mix well, then divide the batter between the 2 mugs.

4 Cook on high for 2 minutes – the mixture may look slightly damp in the middle – then allow to stand for 1 minute.

5 Cool slightly, then run a knife blade around the edge of each cup. Drizzle the ginger syrup over each gingerbread and allow to cool.

6 Remove from the mug and allow to cool completely.

STICKY TOFFEE PUDDING

SERVES 1

Cook/prep time: about 6 minutes, plus cooling

Microwave: 1000W, category-E (see page 5)

FOR THE PUDDING

5 ready-to-eat stoned dates, roughly chopped

1 tbsp boiling water

¼ tsp bicarbonate of soda

1 tbsp softened butter

1 tbsp light muscovado sugar

1 tbsp self-raising flour

½ beaten egg

FOR THE TOFFEE SAUCE

1 tbsp light muscovado sugar

1 tbsp softened butter

1 tbsp crème fraîche

TO SERVE

Vanilla ice cream or custard

A rich and indulgent pudding, drizzled with a simple toffee sauce... this one is perfect for Sunday lunch – although you may need a brisk walk afterwards!

1 Put the dates in the bottom of a 300 ml/ ½ pint microwaveable mug. Add the boiling water and cook on high for 30 seconds. Remove and stir in the bicarbonate of soda; the mixture will fizz. Allow to stand for 30 seconds, then stir to break up the dates.

2 Add the butter to the dates and microwave on high for 10–20 seconds, or until melted. Stir in the sugar, flour and egg and mix well. Microwave on high for 1½ minutes, until risen and spongy. Allow to stand for 1 minute.

3 To make the sauce, put the sugar, butter and crème fraîche in a small microwaveable cup or bowl and microwave on high for 30 seconds. Stir well, then microwave on high for another 30 seconds. Pour over the top of the pudding, pulling away the sides of the sponge so that the sauce can soak through.

4 Serve immediately with vanilla ice cream or custard.

STRAWBERRY BAKED CHEESECAKES

SERVES
2

Prep/cook time: 6 minutes,
plus 2 hours chilling time

Microwave: 1000W, category-E
(see page 5)

2 tbsp butter

4 digestive biscuits, crushed

FOR THE FILLING

½ x 200 g/7 oz tub of cream cheese

4 tbsp crème fraîche or
soured cream

1 tsp vanilla extract

1 tsp finely grated lemon zest

4 tbsp caster sugar

1 egg, beaten

TO DECORATE

Sliced strawberries

Strawberry coulis

*New York-style cheesecake is traditionally cooked slowly
in the oven; however, this method produces a similar
result, with only a small amount of effort and time.
Try it topped with blueberries if you prefer.*

1 Put 1 tbsp of the butter in the bottom of 2 x 200 ml/
7 fl oz microwaveable cups; glass ones are ideal.
Microwave on high for 30 seconds–1 minute,
or until the butter has melted.

2 Divide the biscuit crumbs between the 2 cups, stir
well until mixed together, then press down with the
back of a spoon.

3 Microwave on medium for 1½ minutes, or until
the crumbs start to puff up. Put the cups in the
fridge to chill while you make the filling.

4 In a small bowl, beat together all the filling ingredients.
Divide the filling between the bases, then microwave
on medium for 2½–3 minutes, or until the outsides
are firm, but the centres are slightly wobbly.

5 Allow to cool slightly, then chill in the refrigerator
for 2 hours. Decorate with sliced fresh strawberries
and a drizzle of strawberry coulis to serve.

COFFEE AND WALNUT CAKE

SERVES 1

Prep/cook time: 3 minutes

Microwave: 1000W, category-E (see page 5)

FOR THE CAKE

2 tbsp softened butter, plus extra for greasing

1 tbsp chicory and coffee essence

2 tbsp self-raising flour

2 tbsp soft brown sugar

1 tbsp chopped walnuts

½ beaten egg

FOR THE ICING

2 tbsp mascarpone cheese

1 tbsp icing sugar

½ tsp chicory and coffee essence

TO DECORATE

2 walnut halves

This moist cake is topped with a delicious coffee-flavoured icing and is so quick and easy to make. Whip this cake up for afternoon tea or stick a candle in it for a speedy birthday treat!

1 To make the cake, lightly butter the inside of a small 300 ml/½ pint microwaveable mug. Add the butter and cook on high for 30 seconds-1 minute, or until melted. Stir in all the remaining cake ingredients and mix well.

2 Microwave on high for 1 minute, until risen and spongy. Allow to stand for 1 minute, then if you prefer, remove from the cup and allow to cool.

3 To make the icing, beat together the mascarpone with the icing sugar and chicory and coffee essence until smooth.

4 Spread the top of the cake with the icing and decorate with the walnut halves.

GOLDEN SYRUP PUDDING

SERVES 1

Cook/prep time: 5 minutes

Microwave: 1000W, category-E (see page 5)

2 tbsp softened butter or margarine, plus extra for greasing

2 tbsp golden syrup

½ tsp lemon juice

2 tbsp caster sugar

½ beaten egg

2 tbsp self-raising flour

1 tsp milk

TO SERVE

Ready-made custard

You can easily double the ingredients in this recipe and put it in two mugs to serve two; simply cook it for two more minutes. This is delicious served with ready-made custard.

1 Lightly butter a 300 ml/ ½ pint microwaveable mug. Spoon 1 tbsp of the syrup over the base and add the lemon juice.

2 In a small cup or bowl, cream together the butter and sugar, then beat in the egg. Stir in the flour and milk, then add it to the syrup in the mug.

3 Microwave on high for 2 minutes, until risen and spongy. Drizzle with the remaining syrup and allow to stand for 1 minute before serving.

4 Serve with custard.

CREAMY VANILLA RICE PUDDING

SERVES 1

Prep/cook time: about 15 minutes

Microwave: 1000W, category-E (see page 5)

4 tbsp risotto rice

½ tsp vanilla extract

2 tsp caster sugar

300 ml/½ pint boiling water

100 ml/3½ fl oz evaporated milk

TO SERVE

Jam

Flaked almonds

Instead of using pudding rice, this recipe calls for risotto rice, because it cooks more quickly and has a nice creamy texture. If you'd like to treat yourself to chocolate rice pudding, then at the end of the cooking time simply add four pieces of chopped milk or dark chocolate and stir until melted.

1 Put the rice in the bottom of a large 500 ml/17 fl oz microwaveable mug. Stir in the vanilla, sugar and 100 ml/3½ fl oz of the water. Stand the mug in a shallow microwaveable bowl (in case any of the liquid boils over). Microwave on high for 3 minutes.

2 Sir the rice and add another 100 ml/3½ fl oz of the water. Microwave on medium for a further 3 minutes. Stir in the remaining water and cook on low for 3 minutes.

3 Stir in half of the evaporated milk and cook on low power for 2 minutes. Stir in the remaining milk and cook for a further 2–3 minutes on low, or until the rice is tender.

4 Stand for 2 minutes before serving with a dollop of jam and some flaked almonds sprinkled over the top.

CHOCOLATE ORANGE PUDDING

SERVES 1

Prep/cook time: 4 minutes

Microwave: 1000W, category-E (see page 5)

1 slice white bread, crusts removed

Softened butter, for spreading

6 pieces of dark chocolate, roughly chopped

1 egg

2 tbsp caster sugar

Grated rind of 1 orange

100 ml/3½ fl oz milk

This gooey bread-and-butter pudding is so easy to make. You can vary it by using a flavoured dark chocolate, such as ginger or chilli, or you could try milk chocolate instead.

1 Spread the bread with the butter, then cut it into squares. Arrange in the bottom of a 300 ml/½ pint microwaveable coffee cup. Add the chocolate pieces, nestling them among the pieces of bread.

2 In a small bowl or jug, whisk together the egg, sugar, orange zest and milk, until the sugar has dissolved. Pour this over the bread mixture.

3 Microwave on high for about 1 minute 50 seconds, or until just set. Allow to stand for 1 minute before serving.

CHRISTMAS PUDDING

SERVES 2

Prep/cook time: about 8 minutes

Microwave: 1000W, category-E (see page 5)

2 tbsp softened butter or margarine, plus extra for greasing

2 tbsp soft brown sugar

1 egg

2 tbsp plain flour

1 tsp mixed spice

4 glacé cherries, halved

8 tbsp dried mixed fruit

1 tbsp black treacle

5 tbsp fresh breadcrumbs

1 tbsp brandy, optional

TO SERVE

Brandy butter or cream

Making this fruity pudding in a cup will give it a nice round shape. When you remove it from the microwave, pour over a tablespoon of brandy for extra flavour. You can ignite it just like a traditional pud – just watch your eyebrows.

1 Lightly grease a 300 ml/ ½ pint microwaveable cup. Add the butter and sugar to the cup and cream together, then add the egg, flour and mixed spice and stir until the mixture is smooth.

2 Stir in the cherries, mixed fruit, treacle and breadcrumbs until well combined.

3 Cover the top loosely with cling film, pierce the film with a knife and microwave on medium for 3 ½ minutes. Pour over the brandy, if using.

4 Allow to stand for 3 minutes before turning out and serving with brandy cream.

DRINKS

ULTIMATE HOT CHOCOLATE

SERVES 1

Prep/cook time: 3 minutes

Microwave: 1000W, category-E (see page 5)

200 ml/7 fl oz milk

25 g/1 oz dark or milk chocolate, broken into small pieces

1–2 tsp sugar, to taste, optional

FOR THE TOPPING

Aerosol whipped cream

Small handful of mini marshmallows

Grated chocolate

Got the winter blues? Take off the chill with this indulgent hot chocolate (pictured on page 118). It's also delicious made with flavoured chocolate, such as orange, mint or coffee.

1 Pour the milk into a 300 ml/½ pint microwaveable mug. Cook on high for 1 minute, then add the chocolate and stir well.

2 Return to the microwave and cook on high for a further 30 seconds, or until the chocolate has melted and the drink is hot. Stir well and add sugar to taste.

3 Swirl cream on the top and decorate with the marshmallows and grated chocolate. Enjoy with a long spoon.

HOT-HOT CHOCOLATE

SERVES 1

Prep/cook time: 2 minutes

Microwave: 1000W, category-E (see page 5)

200 ml/7 fl oz full-fat or semi-skimmed milk

Finely grated zest of ½ lime

25 g/1 oz dark chocolate flavoured with chilli, broken into small pieces

Sugar, to taste, optional

This fiery hot chocolate is made simply by using chocolate infused with chilli. You could use dark chocolate mixed with a little hot chilli powder instead. Either way, this is a quick winter warmer with a kick!

1 Pour the milk into a 300 ml/½ pint microwaveable mug and add the lime zest. Cook on high for 1 minute, then add the chocolate.

2 Stir well, then return to the microwave and cook on high for 30 seconds, or until the drink is hot and all the chocolate has melted. Stir again and add sugar to taste.

3 Allow to cool slightly, then enjoy.

MULLED CIDER WITH GINGER

SERVES 1

Prep/cook time: about 3 minutes, plus 5 minutes cooling time

Microwave: 1000W, category-E (see page 5)

200 ml/7 fl oz cider

1 star anise

2 cm/¾-inch piece fresh root ginger, peeled and cut into thin slices

½ small apple, cored and cut into thin slices

1 strip lemon zest

1 tsp demerara sugar

Fresh ginger gives a spicy, warming kick to this cider. For a really festive wintery taste, add a small cinnamon stick, too.

1 Put all the ingredients in a tall 300 ml/½ pint microwaveable glass latte mug. Microwave on high for 1 minute. Stir well, then microwave on high for 40 seconds.

2 Leave to stand for 5 minutes to allow the flavours to infuse and the drink to cool slightly.

VANILLA LATTE

Prep/cook time: 2 minutes

*Microwave: 1000W, category-E
(see page 5)*

2 tsp instant espresso powder

4 tsp boiling water

200 ml/7 fl oz milk

2 tsp vanilla extract

1–2 tsp vanilla sugar, to taste

You can make this breakfast beverage with skimmed milk for a skinny latte – or if you fancy something more indulgent, top it off with a swirl of aerosol cream and a little grated chocolate.

1 Dissolve the coffee in the boiling water in the bottom of a 300 ml/½ pint microwaveable latte cup. Stir in all the remaining ingredients.

2 Microwave on high for 1 minute. Stir well and return to the microwave for 30 seconds.

3 Allow to cool slightly – and enjoy!

CHILL-OUT MILK

SERVES 1

Prep/cook time: 2 minutes

Microwave: 1000W, category-E (see page 5)

200 ml/7 fl oz milk

2 tsp honey

Pinch of ground cinnamon

Pinch of ground nutmeg

A bedtime drink, ideal for helping you to get that elusive perfect night's sleep. Sweet dreams ...

1 Put all the ingredients in a 300 ml/½ pint microwaveable mug.

2 Cook on high for 1 minute, stir well, then return to the microwave and cook for a further 30 seconds until hot.

INDEX